*To my dear Andrew and Noah,
may you benefit from our great Chinese heritage
throughout your lives.*

送给我的宝贝童童和多多,
愿中华文化使你们终身受益。

We acknowledge the financial support of
the Government of Canada through the Book
Publishing Industry Development Program
(BPIDP) for our publishing activities.

Canadä

BILINGUAL SONGS
English-Mandarin Chinese vol. 1

英汉双语歌 第一册

by
许卓 Theresa Xu

Music by Sara Jordan

Produced and Published by
Sara Jordan Publishing
a division of ℗©2009 Jordan Music Productions Inc.
(SOCAN)

ISBN: 978-1-55386-105-8

Acknowledgments

Author, Lyricist - 许卓 Theresa Xu
Editor, Educational Consultant- 杨旸 Eric Yang
Composer and Producer - Sara Jordan
Music Coproducer, Arranger, Engineer - Mark Shannon
Male Singers - 徐常鑫 Steven Xu, Dan Clancy, Ricky Franco
Female Singers - 徐诺 Winona Xunuo, Jennifer Moore
Illustrations - Various contributors
Cover Design - Campbell Creative Services
Interior Layout - Darryl Taylor

Digitally Recorded and Mixed by Mark Shannon,
The TreeFort, Toronto, Ontario, 2008.

For further information contact:

Jordan Music Productions Inc.
M.P.O. Box 490
Niagara Falls, NY
U.S.A. 14302-0490

Jordan Music Productions Inc.
Station M, Box 160
Toronto, Ontario
Canada, M6S 4T3

Internet: http://www.sara-jordan.com
e-mail: sjordan@sara-jordan.com
Telephone: 1-800-567-7733

℗© 2009 Sara Jordan Publishing and
Jordan Music Productions Inc. (SOCAN)
All rights reserved.

For individuals or institutions located in the United States, permission is given to reproduce one set for your classroom purposes.

Reproduction of the whole or any part of this publication is permitted only with the express written permission of the copyright holder, or under a licence from Access Copyright, The Canadian Copyright Licensing Agency or another national reprographic rights organization.

Contents / 目录

    Hints for Teachers and Parents 6

1. Introduction / 简介 8
2. The Alphabet / 字母歌 10
3. Counting to 10 / 数到10 14
4. Days of the Week / 一周的七天 16
5. Months of the Year / 月份歌 20
6. Weather and Seasons / 节气歌 24
7. Colors / 色彩歌 27
8. Food / 食物歌 30
9. The Twelve Chinese Zodiac Signs / 十二生肖歌 34
10. The Body / 身体歌 38
11. Clothing / 服装歌 40
12. Family / 家庭歌 43

Hints for Teachers and Parents

A few ways to use this resource:

Each song can be used to teach either Mandarin or English. Pinyin is also included to aid in pronunciation.

Try lowering the volume of the language being taught to ensure active student participation.

Encourage advanced students to write new lyrics using the music accompaniment tracks.

Encourage students to write down new vocabulary words they have heard in the song.

Entire families can enjoy learning these songs by listening at home or in the car. Try singing along using the lyrics book. Maybe you'll discover a star in your own home!

Please visit our website: www.SongsThatTeach.com to look and listen to our other fabulous resources, to enter contests and tomeet other students around the world.

Sincerely,

Sara Jordan

President

给老师和家长的提示

使用本书的一些方法：

每首歌曲都可以用来教中文或英语。

试着降低教授语言的音量，来保证学生的积极参与。

鼓励优秀学生，使用伴奏带创作新歌词。

当学生听歌听到生词时，鼓励他们写下来。

全家可在家中或车上一起听歌，享受学习乐趣。不妨仅看歌词单独唱下，没准你家就有明星！

更多精彩资源，敬请访问我们的网站：www.SongsThatTeach.com，还可参与竞赛，与来自各国的学生交流。

此致，
Sara Jordan
总裁

Nº 1

Introduction
简介

Hello my friends.
It is time to sing with me.
"Bilingual Songs, Volume 1"
makes learning fun. You will see.

朋 友 们 你 们 好,
péng you men nǐ men hǎo,

请 随 我 一 齐 唱。
qǐng suí wǒ yì qí chàng。

双 语 歌, 第 一 册,
shuāng yǔ gē, dì yī cè,

学 语 言, 更 快 乐。
xué yǔ yán, gèng kuài lè。

You will be surprised
at how much learning there can be.
What a chance! Sing and dance
with "Bilingual Songs, Volume 1".

> 你不要惊奇,
> nǐ bú yào jīng qí,
>
> 多少知识可以学习。
> duō shǎo zhī shi kě yǐ xué xí。
>
> 唱和跳, 多快乐!
> chàng hé tiào, duō kuài lè!
>
> 只需双语歌, 第一册。
> zhǐ xū shuāng yǔ gē, dì yī cè。

What a chance! Sing and dance
with "Bilingual Songs, Volume 1".

> 唱和跳, 多快乐!
> chàng hé tiào, duō kuài lè!
>
> 只需双语歌, 第一册。
> zhǐ xū shuāng yǔ gē, dì yī cè。

Nº 2

The Alphabet
字母歌

chorus/反复:

The Mandarin pinyin sounds
are easy. You will see.
When we sing together
Mandarin is easy.

英语的字母啊，
yīng yǔ de zì mǔ a,

多简单试试看。
duō jiǎn dān shì shì kàn。

当我们一起唱，
dāng wǒ men yì qǐ chàng,

学习英语多简单。
xué xí yīng yǔ duō jiǎn dān。

A B C D E F G

H I J K

L M N O P

Q R S T U Ü

W X Y 和 Z

今 天 学 会 念 拼 音。
jīn tiān xué huì niàn pīn yīn。

简 简 单 单 别 担 心。
jiǎn jiǎn dān dān bié dān xīn。

A B C D E F G

H I J K

L M N O P

Q R S T U V

W X Y Z

Now I know my A B Cs.
It's so easy. You can see.

Did you know?
你知道吗？

Hanyu Pinyin is used to spell the sounds of Mandarin words using letters that are almost the same as the ones in the English alphabet.

Even though the letters may look the same, they sound very different. Instead of using vowels and consonants to form words, Pinyin uses 17 initials and 37 finals. These groups, of one or more letters, can be combined to form Mandarin words.

There are even five different tones that change the way the final is pronounced. There is no letter V in Pinyin, instead there is a U-umlaut (Ü).

英语有26个字母，其中21个辅音字母和5个元音字母。元音字母在不同单词中，有长短发音之分，但没有声调。

Nº 3

Counting to 10
数 到 十

chorus/反复 2x:

I can count.
    我 会 数。
    wǒ huì shǔ。

You can count.
    你 会 数。
    nǐ huì shǔ。

We can count.
    我 们 会 数。
    wǒ men huì shǔ。

Count!
    数！
    shǔ!

One, two, three, four, five,
six, seven, eight, nine, ten.

一, 二, 三, 四, 五,
yī, èr, sān, sì, wǔ,

六, 七, 八, 九, 十。
liù, qī, bā, jiǔ, shí。

One, two, three,

一, 二, 三,
yī, èr, sān,

four, five, six,
四, 五, 六,
sì, wǔ, liù,

seven, eight,
七, 八,
qī, bā,

nine and ten.
九 和 十。
jiǔ hé shí。

One, two, three, four, five,
six, seven, eight, nine, ten.

一, 二, 三, 四, 五,
yī, èr, sān, sì, wǔ,

六, 七, 八, 九, 十。
liù, qī, bā, jiǔ, shí。

N° 4

Days of the Week
一周的七天

chorus/反复 2x:

Let's sing the days of the week!
我们来唱 一周的七天!
wǒ men lái chàng yì zhōu de qī tiān!

Let's sing the days of the week!
我们来唱 一周的七天!
wǒ men lái chàng yì zhōu de qī tiān!

Sunday   周 日
              zhōu rì

Monday   周 一
              zhōu yī

Tuesday   周 二
              zhōu èr

Wednesday   周 三
              zhōu sān

Thursday   周 四
              zhōu sì

Friday	周 五
	zhōu wǔ

Saturday	周 六
	zhōu liù

LET'S SING! 一 起 唱!
　　　　　　yì qǐ chàng!

chorus/反复:

Let's sing the days of the week!
　　我 们 来 唱 一 周 的 七 天!
　　wǒ men lái chàng yì zhōu de qī tiān!

Let's sing the days of the week!
　　我 们 来 唱 一 周 的 七 天!
　　wǒ men lái chàng yì zhōu de qī tiān!

Sunday	周 日
	zhōu rì

Monday	周 一
	zhōu yī

Tuesday	周 二
	zhōu èr

Wednesday	周 三	zhōu sān
Thursday	周 四	zhōu sì
Friday	周 五	zhōu wǔ
Saturday	周 六	zhōu liù
LET'S SING!	一起 唱!	yì qǐ chàng!

chorus/反复 2x:

Let's sing the days of the week!
我 们 来 唱 一 周 的 七 天!
wǒ men lái chàng yì zhōu de qī tiān!

Let's sing the days of the week!
我 们 来 唱 一 周 的 七 天!
wǒ men lái chàng yì zhōu de qī tiān!

Did you know?
你知道吗？

In the Chinese calendar year, each week begins on a Monday. There are two words that Mandarin speakers use for week; 星期 (xīngqī) or 周 (zhōu) which really means cycle.

Each day, except Sunday, has a number instead of a name. Monday is 周一 (zhōu yī) for week 1, Tuesday is 周二 (zhōu èr) for week 2, Wednesday is 周三 (zhōu sān) for week 3, Thursday is 周四 (zhōu sì) for week 4, Friday is 周五 (zhōu wǔ) for week 5, Saturday is 周六 (zhōu liù) for week 6 and Sunday is 周日 (zhōu rì) which really means week "day".

多数英语国家的日历上，周日是每周的第一天。一周的七天以太阳，月亮，和其他日耳曼诸神命名。显而易见，周日和周一分别以太阳和月亮命名。周二则是以战争之神 Tiw 命名，周三以 Woden 命名，周四是 Thor, 周五为 Frigg (或 Freyja), 周六之名则源自行星土星。

Nº 5

Months of the Year
月份歌

chorus/反复：

January, February,
March, April, May,
June, July,
August, September,
October, November
and December.

一月份，二月份，
yī yuè fèn, èr yuè fèn,

三月，四月，五月，
sān yuè, sì yuè, wǔ yuè,

六月，七月，
liù yuè, qī yuè,

八月，九月，
bā yuè, jiǔ yuè,

十月，十一月，
shí yuè, shí yī yuè,

还有十二月。
hái yǒu shí èr yuè。

Each year has twelve months
but my birhday only happens once.
So my favorite month of all
is the one where my birthday falls.

每年都有十二月，
měi nián dōu yǒu shí èr yuè,

我的生日却只有一次。
wǒ de shēng rì què zhǐ yǒu yí cì。

我最喜欢的那个月，
wǒ zuì xǐ huān de nà gè yuè,

就是我生日的那月。
jiù shì wǒ shēng rì de nà yuè。

chorus/反复:

January, February,
March, April, May,
June, July,
August, September,
October, November
and December.

一月份，二月份，
yī yuè fèn, èr yuè fèn,

三月，四月，五月，
sān yuè, sì yuè, wǔ yuè,

六月，七月，
liù yuè, qī yuè,

八月，九月，
bā yuè, jiǔ yuè,

十月，十一月，
shí yuè, shí yī yuè,

还有十二月。
hái yǒu shí èr yuè。

Months of the Year
一年的月份

January	一月	yī yuè
February	二月	èr yuè
March	三月	sān yuè
April	四月	sì yuè
May	五月	wǔ yuè
June	六月	liù yuè
July	七月	qī yuè
August	八月	bā yuè
September	九月	jiǔ yuè
October	十月	shí yuè
November	十一月	shí yī yuè
December	十二月	shí èr yuè

N° 6

Weather and Seasons
节 气 歌

How's the weather? Is it hot?
    天 气 怎 样？热 不 热？
    tiān qì zěn yàng? rè bú rè?

In summer the temperature's hotter.
    夏 天，天 会 更 热。
    xià tiān, tiān huì gèng rè。

How's the weather? Is it cold?
    天 气 怎 样？冷 不 冷？
    tiān qì zěn yàng? lěng bù lěng?

In winter the temperature's colder.
    冬 天，天 会 更 冷。
    dōng tiān, tiān huì gèng lěng。

chorus/反复：

Autumn and winter, spring and summer,
we love all the seasons the year has to offer.
    秋 天 和 冬 天,
    qiū tiān hé dōng tiān,

    春 天 和 夏 天,
    chūn tiān hé xià tiān,

    一 年 四 季 我 们
    yì nián sì jì wǒ men

    全 都 喜 欢。
    quán dōu xǐ huān。

How's the weather? Is it mild?
    天 气 怎 样？ 暖 不 暖？
    tiān qì zěn yàng？ nuǎn bù nuǎn？

In springtime the temperature's milder.
    春 天 时， 天 气 更 暖。
    chūn tiān shí, tiān qì gèng nuǎn。

How's the weather? Is it windy?
    天 气 怎 样？ 有 风 吗？
    tiān qì zěn yàng？ yǒu fēng ma？

In autumn the wind blows stronger.
秋 天 时， 风 刮 更 大。
qiū tiān shí, fēng guā gèng dà。

chorus/反复：

Autumn and winter, spring and summer,
we love all the seasons the year has to offer.
秋 天 和 冬 天,
qiū tiān hé dōng tiān,

春 天 和 夏 天,
chūn tiān hé xià tiān,

一 年 四 季 我 们
yì nián sì jì wǒ men

全 都 喜 欢。
quán dōu xǐ huān。

Nº 7

Colors
色彩歌

chorus/反复：

I like to eat jelly beans. It's fun!
Which color is your favorite one?
　　我 喜 欢　吃吉利 豆。 多　快 乐！
　　wǒ xǐ huān chī jí lì dòu。 duō kuài lè!

　　哪一　 种　 颜 色你最喜 欢？
　　nǎ yì zhǒng yán sè nǐ zuì xǐ huān?

Red, yellow, purple, white,
green, pink, blue; you choose!
　　红 色,　黄　色, 紫色, 白,
　　hóng sè, huáng sè, zǐ sè, bái,

　　绿色, 粉 色, 蓝; 你　选　一个！
　　lǜ sè, fěn sè, lán; nǐ xuǎn yí gè!

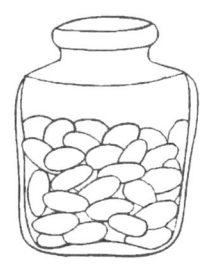

I like orange.
我 喜 欢 橙 色。
wǒ xǐ huān chéng sè。

I don't like purple.
我 不 喜 欢 紫色。
wǒ bù xǐ huān zǐ sè。

I like yellow.
我 喜 欢 黄 色。
wǒ xǐ huān huáng sè。

I don't like white.
我 不 喜 欢 白 色。
wǒ bù xǐ huān bái sè。

I like green.
我 喜 欢 绿色。
wǒ xǐ huān lǜ sè。

I don't like blue.
我 不 喜 欢 蓝 色。
wǒ bù xǐ huān lán sè。

I like pink.
我 喜 欢 粉 色。
wǒ xǐ huān fěn sè。

How about you?
你 呢？
nǐ ne？

chorus/反复:

I like to eat jelly beans. It's fun!
Which color is your favorite one?
我 喜 欢 吃吉利豆。 多 快 乐!
wǒ xǐ huān chī jí lì dòu。 duō kuài lè!

哪 一 种 颜 色 你 最 喜 欢?
nǎ yì zhǒng yán sè nǐ zuì xǐ huān?

Red, yellow, purple, white,
green, pink, blue; you choose!
红 色, 黄 色,紫色,白,
hóng sè, huáng sè, zǐ sè, bái,

绿色, 粉 色, 蓝;你 选 一 个!
lǜ sè, fěn sè, lán; nǐ xuǎn yí gè!

Colors
颜色

orange	橙色	chéng sè
yellow	黄色	huáng sè
purple	紫色	zǐ sè
white	白色	bái sè
green	绿色	lǜ sè
pink	粉红	fěn hóng
blue	蓝色	lán sè

Nº 8

Food
食物歌

chorus/反复：

I feel hungry, very, very hungry.
I feel hungry, very, very hungry.
    我 好饿, 非 常， 非 常 饿。
    wǒ hǎo è, fēi cháng， fēi cháng è。

    我 好饿, 非 常， 非 常 饿。
    wǒ hǎo è, fēi cháng， fēi cháng è。

We need milk. We need bread.
We need eggs early this morning.
    我 们 要 牛 奶， 要 面 包。
    wǒ men yào niú nǎi, yào miàn bāo。

    今 天 的 一 早 我 们 要 鸡 蛋。
    jīn tiān de yì zǎo wǒ men yào jī dàn。

Rice and noodles and some peas.
Something for the dumpling if you please.
　　米 饭 面 条, 还 有 豆 子。
　　mǐ fàn miàn tiáo, hái yǒu dòu zi。

　　如 果 可 以 还 有 饺 子。
　　rú guǒ kě yǐ hái yǒu jiǎo zi。

We need orange juice. We need coffee,
soda pop, and we need tea.
　　我 们 要 橙 汁。要 咖 啡,
　　wǒ men yào chéng zhī。yào kā fēi,

　　要 汽 水, 还 有 茶 水。
　　yào qì shuǐ, hái yǒu chá shuǐ。

We need meat and celery.
We need carrots and broccoli.
　　　我 们 要 肉，还 有 芹 菜。
　　　wǒ men yào ròu, hái yǒu qín cài。

　　　胡 萝 卜，还 有 西 兰 花。
　　　hú luó bo, hái yǒu xī lán huā。

chorus/反复：

I feel hungry, very, very hungry.
I feel hungry, very, very hungry.
　　　我 好 饿，非 常， 非 常 饿。
　　　wǒ hǎo è, fēi cháng, fēi cháng è。

　　　我 好 饿，非 常， 非 常 饿。
　　　wǒ hǎo è, fēi cháng, fēi cháng è。

Nº 9

The Twelve Chinese Zodiac Signs
十二生肖歌

chorus/反复:

The Chinese zodiac's based on the moon,
中国生肖源自月，
zhōng guó shēng xiāo yuán zì yuè,

with a lunar calendar sixty years long.
一轮阴历有六十年。
yì lún yīn lì yǒu liù shí nián。

We'll learn twelve animal signs
这首歌曲可以学
zhè shǒu gē qǔ kě yǐ xué

and five basic elements with this song.
十二生肖五元素。
shí èr shēng xiāo wǔ yuán sù。

The rat, ox and tiger,
rabbit, dragon, snake and horse,
the ram, and the monkey,
rooster, dog, and pig, of course.

老鼠，牛，和老虎，
lǎo shǔ, niú, hé lǎo hǔ,

兔子，龙，蛇和马，
tù zi, lóng, shé hé mǎ,

羊，和猴子，
yáng, hé hóu zi,

公鸡，还有狗和猪。
gōng jī, hái yǒu gǒu hé zhū。

chorus/反复：

There are five basic elements
combined with the animal signs.
Metal, wood, water, fire,
and earth are things we'll memorize.

总 共 有 五 种 基 本 元 素
zǒng gòng yǒu wǔ zhǒng jī běn yuán sù

结 合 十 二 种 动 物。
jié hé shí èr zhǒng dòng wù。

金，木，水，火，土，
jīn, mù, shǔi, huǒ, tǔ,

我 们 要 记 住。
wǒ men yào jì zhù。

chorus/反复：

On elements and animal signs
the Chinese zodiac depends.
The lunar cycle is sixty years
at which time it starts again.

元 素 和 动 物
yuán sù hé dòng wù

决 定 了 生 肖。
jué dìng le shēng xiāo。

阴 历 轮 回 六 十 年,
yīn lì lún huí liù shí nián,

到 时 会 再 次 开 始。
dào shí huì zài cì kāi shǐ。

chorus/反复:

N° 10

The Body*
身体歌**

sing 2x / 唱 2x :

Touch your head.
     碰　碰　你 的　头。
     pèng pèng nǐ de tóu。

Touch your shoulders.
     碰　碰　你 的　肩。
     pèng pèng nǐ de jiān。

Touch your feet.
     碰　碰　你 的　脚。
     pèng pèng nǐ de jiǎo。

Touch your knees.
     碰　碰　你 的　膝。
     pèng pèng nǐ de xī。

Touch your eyes.
     碰　碰　你 的　眼。
     pèng pèng nǐ de yǎn。

Touch your ears.
　　碰　碰　你的 耳。
　　pèng pèng nǐ de ěr。

Touch your mouth,
　　碰　碰　你的 嘴,
　　pèng pèng nǐ de zuǐ,

nose and cheeks.
　　鼻子 和 脸　蛋。
　　bí zi hé liǎn dàn。

Head, shoulders, feet and knees,
eyes, ears, mouth, nose and cheeks.
　　头, 肩　膀,　脚, 膝 盖,
　　tóu, jiān bǎng, jiǎo, xī gài,

　　眼, 耳, 嘴, 鼻子 和　脸　蛋。
　　yǎn, ěr, zuǐ, bí zi hé liǎn dàn。

* The entire song is sung twice through.
** 整首歌曲请唱两遍。

Clothing
服装歌

chorus/反复：

When I wake up in the morning
I brush my hair,
wash my face and
decide what to wear.

当 我 早 上 一 觉 醒 来,
dāng wǒ zǎo shàng yí jiào xǐng lái,

我 梳 梳 头,
wǒ shū shū tóu,

又 洗 洗 脸,
yòu xǐ xǐ liǎn,

决 定 穿 什 么。
jué dìng chuān shén me。

I'll wear a skirt.
我 穿 裙 子。
wǒ chuān qún zi。

I'll wear some pants.
我 穿 裤 子。
wǒ chuān kù zi。

I'll wear some shoes.
　　我　穿　鞋。
　　wǒ chuān xié。

I'll wear some socks.
　　我　穿　袜。
　　wǒ chuān wà。

chorus/反复：

I'll wear a blouse.
　　我　穿　上　衣。
　　wǒ chuān shàng yī。

I'll wear a shirt.
　　我　穿　衬　衫。
　　wǒ chuān chèn shān。

I'll wear a sweater.
　　我　穿　毛　衣。
　　wǒ chuān máo yī。

I'll wear a jacket.
　　我　穿　夹　克。
　　wǒ chuān jiá kè。

chorus/反复:

I'll wear a hat.
    我 戴 帽 子。
    wǒ dài mào zi。

I'll wear a raincoat.
    我 穿 雨 衣。
    wǒ chuān yǔ yī。

I'll wear some boots.
    我 穿 靴 子。
    wǒ chuān xuē zi。

Are you ready? Let's go!
    你 准 备 好 了? 出 发!
    nǐ zhǔn bèi hǎo le? chū fā!

chorus/反复:

Nº 12

Family
家庭歌

chorus/反复：

Hi, friend! Let's invite our families
to have a picnic by the lake.
So much food. So many people.
What a great meal we will make.

  嗨，朋友！让我们邀请家人
  hài, péng you! ràng wǒ men yāo qǐng jiā rén

  来到湖边聚个餐。
  lái dào hú biān jù gè cān。

  多少食物，多少人，
  duō shǎo shí wù, duō shǎo rén,

  我们会有多好的一顿饭。
  wǒ men huì yǒu duō hǎo de yí dùn fàn。

Let's make a list:
  我们列个单子：
  wǒ men liè gè dān zi:

My mother,	我母亲,	wǒ mǔ qīn,
father,	父亲,	fù qīn,
sister,	姐姐,	jiě jie,
brother,	哥哥,	gē ge,
grandmother,	外祖母,	wài zǔ mǔ,
grandfather.	外祖父。	wài zǔ fù。

这 是 我 的 单 子:
zhè shì wǒ de dān zi:

Here is my list:

我母亲,	wǒ mǔ qīn,	My mother,
继父,	jì fù,	step-father,
哥哥,	gē ge,	brother,
叔叔,	shū shu,	uncle,
阿姨,	ā yí,	aunt,
和表兄。	hé biǎo xiōng。	and cousins.

chorus/反复:

Hi, friend! Let's invite our families
to have a picnic by the lake.
So much food. So many people.
What a great meal we will make.

嗨，朋友！让我们邀请家人
hài, péng you! ràng wǒ men yāo qǐng jiā rén

来到湖边聚个餐。
lái dào hú biān jù gè cān。

多少食物，多少人，
duō shǎo shí wù, duō shǎo rén,

我们会有多好的一顿饭。
wǒ men huì yǒu duō hǎo de yí dùn fàn。

Ask your retailer about other excellent audio programs by teacher, Sara Jordan

Bilingual Preschool™

Jump-start learning for preschoolers as they sing and participate in these bilingual songs and games including I Spy, Follow the Leader and Mind Your Manners. This kit teaches: names of animals, counting, directions, polite expressions, places in the community, and counting (cardinal and ordinal numbers). Sung by native speakers, these bilingual songs are a perfect introduction to the new language.
ENGLISH-FRENCH and ENGLISH-SPANISH

Bilingual Songs™ Volumes 1-4

*** Parents'   Choice Award Winner! ***

The perfect way to have fun while acquiring a second language. This series teaches the basic alphabet, counting to 100, days of the week, months of the year, colors, food, animals, parts of the body, clothing, family members, emotions, places in the community and the countryside, measurement, opposites, greetings, gender, articles, plural forms of nouns, adjectives, pronouns, adverbs of frequency, question words and much more!
ENGLISH-FRENCH and ENGLISH-SPANISH

Songs and Activities for Early Learners™

Dynamic songs teach the alphabet, counting, parts of the body, members of the family, colors, shapes, fruit and more. Helps students of all ages to learn basic vocabulary easily. The kit includes a lyrics book with activities which teachers may reproduce for their classes.
IN ENGLISH, FRENCH OR SPANISH

Thematic Songs for Learning Language™

Delightful collection of songs and activities teaching salutations, rooms of the house, pets, meals, food and silverware, transportation, communication, parts of the body, clothing, weather and prepositions. Great for ESL classes. The kit includes a lyrics book with activities which teachers may reproduce for their classes.
IN ENGLISH, FRENCH OR SPANISH

Reading Readiness™ Songs

Packaged with a lyrics book which includes helpful hints for parents and teachers. This great introduction to reading uses both phonetic and whole language approaches. Topics covered include the alphabet, vowels, consonants, telling time, days of the week, seasons, the environment and more!
VERSIONS IN ENGLISH, FRENCH OR SPANISH

Grammar Grooves vol.1™

Ten songs that teach about nouns, pronouns, adjectives, verbs, tenses, adverbs and punctuation. Activities and puzzles, which may be reproduced, are included in the lyrics book to help reinforce learning even further. A complement of music tracks to the 10 songs is included for karaoke performances. Also great for music night productions.
IN ENGLISH, FRENCH OR SPANISH

Funky Phonics®: Learn to Read Volumes 1-4

Blending the best in educational research and practice, Sara Jordan's four part series provides students with the strategies needed to decode words through rhyming, blending and segmenting. Teachers and parents love the lessons while children will find the catchy, toe-tapping tunes fun.
IN ENGLISH

Singing Sight Words Volumes 1-4

This collection of fun songs builds a solid foundation for all beginning readers. By incorporating Dolch sight words into memorable and catchy melodies, early readers are quickly able to recognize the more common and basic words found in age-appropriate literature. IN ENGLISH

Lullabies Around the World

*** Parents' Choice Award Winner! ***

Traditional lullabies sung by native singers with translated verses in English. Multicultural activities are included in the lyrics book. Includes a complement of music tracks for class performances.
Pre-K - Grade 3   11 DIFFERENT LANGUAGES

The Math Unplugged™ Series

Available for Addition, Subtraction, Division and Multiplication. Tuneful songs teach kids the basic math facts. Repetitive, musical and fun. A great resource. Each audio kit includes a lyrics book with worksheet pages which may be reproduced.
IN ENGLISH

Check out these great Resource Books full of reproducible activities and exercises for the classroom.

Bilingual Kids™ Volumes 1-4

Reproducible, black-line, thematic lessons and exercises, based on *Bilingual Songs*, teach the basic alphabet, counting to 100, days of the week, months of the year, colors, food, animals, parts of the body, clothing, family members, emotions, places in the community and the countryside, measurement, opposites, greetings, gender, articles, plural forms of nouns, adjectives, pronouns, adverbs of frequency, question words and much more! ENGLISH-FRENCH and ENGLISH-SPANISH

Funky Phonics®: Learn to Read Volumes 1-4

Reproducible, black-line, thematic lessons and exercises, based on the *Funky Phonics®: Learn to Read* audio series, is a structured program providing students with the strategies needed to decode words. Teachers, parents and beginning readers love the lessons, hands on activities and reproducible worksheets. IN ENGLISH

Learning Sight Words Volumes 1-4

This four-part series of 64 page, reproducible, resource/activity books teaches students 300 of the most commonly used sight words. The words are presented in order of frequency and are based on the 200 most frequently used service words compiled by Edward William Dolch, Ph.D., and the related list of 95 high-frequency nouns. It is estimated that 50-75% of all words used in school books, library books, newspapers and magazines are included in the Dolch Basic Sight Vocabulary. This series can be used independently or in tandem with the audio/book series Singing Sight Words. IN ENGLISH

Please visit our English and Spanish websites, great meeting places for kids, teachers and parents on the Internet.
www.SongsThatTeach.com
www.AprendeCantando.com
For help finding a retailer near you contact Sara Jordan Publishing 1-800-567-7733